The New England COUNTRY TAVERN

Jack Larkin

Printed in the United States of America

Library of Congress Cataloging-in-Publication Data

Larkin, Jack, 1943-
  The New England country tavern / by Jack Larkin.
      p. cm.
Includes bibliographical references.
  ISBN 0-913387-05-3
  1. New England-Social life and customs–19th century. 2. Taverns (Inns)–New England–History–19th century. 3. Country life–New England–History–19th century. I. Title.
  F8 .L37 2000
  641.9574'09034-dc21

                                        00-010178

ON THE COVER: Monochrome wall painting c. 1830, artist unknown, Oliver Wight House, Old Sturbridge Village (Lodges).

An Old Sturbridge Village Publication

Foreword

For more than a half century, Old Sturbridge Village has brought early New England to life in the seasonal work, play, and celebrations of "ordinary" people — blacksmiths and farmers, printers and potters, innkeepers and itinerant singing masters. More than 21 million visitors have stepped back in time to explore our country roads and rolling hills, a world in which we preserve the special rhythms and values of earlier times.

Along with historically costumed staff and restored historic New England structures, this scenic landscape tells the story of an era of important change. During the early years of our nation (1790-1840), Americans saw their world being transformed by the forces of growth, discovery, invention, emerging technology, and social reform.

Much of the discussion and debate surrounding such change took place where New Englanders gathered to socialize, to learn the latest news, seeking recreation, relaxation, good Yankee dining, and even entertainment. New England taverns — as plentiful in the countryside as omnipresent white-steepled meetinghouses — served as their main gateway to a widening world of travel, commerce, communication, and socialization.

In *The New England Country Tavern*, drawing upon the Village's vast collections of early artifacts and years of research, Chief Historian Jack Larkin takes a look at the important role these gathering places played in directing the communal affairs of a new young nation. His journey is one of discovery and excitement, of gaining a greater understanding of a history we have long taken for granted.

Education is at the foundation of our democracy; preservation is at the heart of our museum's mission. Exploring the world of early nineteenth-century taverns is one more way we can re-create the sights, sounds, smells, tastes, and textures of old New England for our visitors; it's also one more way to give new dimension and greater meaning to both the present and the future.

Alberta Sebolt George

Alberta Sebolt George
President, Old Sturbridge Village

Taverns have a long history in New England. Places of accommodation for travelers appeared within a few years of the founding of Boston in 1630, and the region's first legislation governing "ordinaries" or "licensed houses" dates to Massachusetts Bay in 1647. Over time they became highly important institutions — vital to community life and essential to travel, communication, and the transportation of goods. [1]

Although it pained New England clergymen to admit it, in the early nineteenth century taverns were as numerous as meetinghouses. The swinging, creaking tavern sign and the meetinghouse steeple were the two most visible signs of community life. In virtually every town there was a "licensed house" sitting on the common at the very center of the community, and outside the villages travelers could find numerous roadside taverns on important highways. Counting both village and countryside, most towns could claim at least two taverns; in larger places there were often two or three competing establishments within a few hundred yards of each other.

Taverns and Travel

From the very beginning, taverns were places where travelers could find a meal and a bed, fodder their horses, and rest from an arduous day on the road. With the great expansion of stagecoach lines after 1790, they came to play an even more crucial role in the

This 1838 view looks down the Worcester-Stafford Turnpike toward the center of Sturbridge, Massachusetts. At the end of the road and to the left is the town's largest tavern, Bullard's Hotel (still in operation today as the Publick House). The Congregational and Baptist Meetinghouses are visible to the right of center. The Baptist Meetinghouse, with its Greek Revival pillars, is now the Center Meetinghouse at Old Sturbridge Village. Wood engraving in John Warner Barber, Massachusetts Historical Collections (Boston, 1839).

transportation system. Many establishments became "stage taverns" — way stations on a stage route where the coaches would stop to change horses and the passengers would eat and rest.

literally hundreds of stage lines, as well as information about steamboat and (after 1835) railway connections. After 1820, the great majority of overnight guests in New England taverns were stagecoach passengers. [2]

Hundreds of New England tavern-keepers doubled as stage company agents. In their stables they kept two or three relays of coach horses — one set resting from the previous day's exertions, another longer-rested and "fresh" for a new start — often along with a spare coach or two. Tavern-keepers posted the stage schedules in their parlors and taprooms and kept copies of *Badger and Porter's Stage Register* — an updated edition came out every two months — to be consulted by their patrons. In the *Register's* pages after 1822 travelers could find the schedules and stopping points of

Although stage schedules were not as exacting as railway timetables later became, they did rush travelers along. This was particularly true for "mail stages," which carried letters under government contract and were held accountable for timely delivery to the post offices along their routes. From the passengers' point of view, tavern stops were all too often short and hurried. "The stage was to leave at four o'clock in the morning," wrote Caroline Fitch about her trip to New Hampshire in 1836, "and this idea was to haunt our broken slumbers. We retired to bed early and often looked at the watch during the night to know how time sped notwithstanding the hours were marked by the striking of the town clock. At three we could endure this tortured sleep no longer we arose and hardly were the duties of the toilette ended ere the stage was at the door." [3]

PROVIDENCE

AND SOUTHBRIDGE,

Accommodation Stage.

A Stage will leave the Manufacturers Hotel, Tuesdays, Thursdays, and Saturdays, at 11 o'clock, A. M. and arrive at Fishersville Depot in time to meet the Cars for Worcester and Norwich, passing the villages of Greenville, Chepachet, Thompson, Masonville, Fishersville, and from thence to New-Boston and Southbridge.

Returning,

Will leave Southbridge Mondays, Wednesdays, and Fridays, at 6 o'clock, A. M. and arrive at Fishersville Depot in time for the morning Cars for Worcester, and Norwich, and arrive at Providence at 1 o'clock, P. M., in time for the Boston, Taunton, and New Bedford Cars, and the Woonsocket, Pawtucket, Bristol, Warwick, and Coventry Stages.

Passengers,

For Killingly, Pomfret, Woodstock, Dudley, Webster, Oxford, Charlton, Sturbridge, Brimfield, Munson, and Palmer, can be accommodated by this Line, cheaper than by any other Line.

Passengers wishing to go to any of the above named places, will find it to their advantage to call on the subscriber at the Manufacturers Hotel, Providence.

J. M. KENSIE, *Driver.*

Stage lines connected the New England countryside to the cities on regular schedules. By the late 1830s, stage lines also made connections with the emerging railways. Taverns were the crucial way stations for this early nineteenth-century transportation system. "Providence and Southbridge Accommodation Stage," Broadside, Old Sturbridge Village Research Library.

The house of Moses Marcy of Sturbridge, Massachusetts, is shown against a fanciful landscape of seacoast, island, and sailing ship. In the foreground, a figure (probably not Marcy) holds a goblet and displays a long-stemmed clay pipe, punchbowl, and ledger book — symbols of commerce and conviviality in New England. Overmantel panel, oil on wood, c. 1775, Old Sturbridge Village collections.

Taverns and the Law

Because they dealt with the entertainment of strangers and the serving of strong drink, taverns were among the most highly regulated of early American enterprises. Across New England, "innholders" or "taverners" had to be certified by the selectmen of their town as men "of good character" before they could be licensed by the county authorities. Yale's president Timothy Dwight praised these stringent requirements in 1800; they accounted, he claimed, for the fact that New England tavernkeepers were far more prosperous, more respectable, and of a higher standing in the community than their counterparts anywhere else. [4]

Under the early nineteenth-century statute law of the New England states, taverns were strictly bound by a mesh of regulations that had changed little since the late seventeenth century. Once a tavernkeeper had been approved by the selectmen and county court, received his license, and put up his sign, he was bound by law to per-form his function. An innholder could be prosecuted for "refusing to make suitable provision when desired, for the receiving of strangers, travelers or others, and their horses and cattle, or for any public entertainment"; if convicted, he would lose his license and have his sign taken down by the sheriff. A tavernkeeper could not serve strong drink to minors or servants — except to those traveling with their masters, who were assumed to be responsible for them. Other restrictions on patrons applied as well. Town selectmen were instructed to identify notorious drunkards who were "wasting their estates" and to order tavernkeepers not to serve them. Nor, in the eyes of the law, could alcoholic beverages be sold on credit or "trust"; in order to keep tavern bills from mounting to ruinous heights, innkeepers were barred from using legal process to collect such debts. [5]

Sabbath regulations also bore hard on tavern operations. On the Lord's Day, innholders were barred from admitting local customers or new traveling guests; they could feed and lodge only those already staying on the prem-

A New England tavern was identified by the innkeeper's name painted on his sign, sometimes along with a decorative figure such as an eagle, a hunting dog, or a rising sun. Taverns were required by law to mount such signs and could be heavily fined for failing to do so. Tavern signs, painted wood, c. 1820-1850, Old Sturbridge Village collections.

ises. Over a longer stretch of time that included both the Sabbath day and the Saturday evening previous, they could not serve drinks or admit those intending to "play or loiter." In law, at least, tavern Sabbath infractions were heavily punished. In the 1830s fines began at $5 to $10. Continued violations of Sabbath restrictions by a tavern-keeper would result in progressively heavier fines and eventual loss of license.

Taverns, Public Houses, Inns, and Hotels

The institutions we are discussing went by a variety of names in both England and America. "Inn" and "public house" (later shortened to "pub") were the terms most frequently used in England. They could be found in America as well, although less commonly. By the 1830s a new appellation, "hotel," was gaining popularity in New England, probably because it conveyed a more genteel image of abundant food and gracious lodging. But the most

widely used term of all in New England was "tavern," which had come into the English language from French in the thirteenth century. In old England, "tavern" usually meant an establishment solely for drinking; but in New England, Webster's *Dictionary* for 1831 declared, "tavern is synonymous with inn or hotel, and denotes a house for the entertainment of travelers as well as for the sale of liquours." This naming pattern is borne out in other evidence as well. In 1831 all the towns of Massachusetts were required to have maps made naming and locating their most important features. Eighty-four establishments could be located on the fifty-five town maps of Worcester County, Massachusetts. Two of them

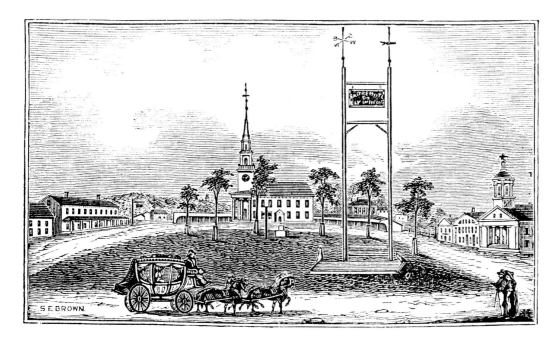

S.E. BROWN.

New England tavern signs were of imposing height, so that they could be seen easily from a distance and read from horseback or the driver's seat of a stagecoach. This one on the common in Barre, Massachusetts, is a particularly dramatic example.
Wood engraving in John Warner Barber, Massachusetts Historical Collections *(Boston, 1839).*

were called "houses of entertainment," six were "public houses," seventeen were "inns," twenty-two were "hotels," and thirty-seven were "taverns." [6]

Tavern Signs

Tavern signs were a widespread and distinctive feature of the New England landscape. Since 1647 they had been required by law, when Massachusetts decreed that every establishment "shall have some inoffensive sign, obvious, for the direction of strangers" posted within three months of its licensing.

Signs customarily stood near the tavern's entrance or directly across the road from it and served to attract the attention of travelers and let them know where beds, food, drink, and animal fodder could be obtained. Local taverngoers, of course, did not need a sign to find the tavern; outside the cities, few purely local establishments such as craftsmen's shops and stores ever used them. Landscape paintings and drawings, and a few very early photographs, tell us that early and mid-nineteenth-century signs were of imposing height, so that they could be

seen easily from a distance and read from horseback or the driver's seat of a stagecoach. [7]

English taverns customarily had fanciful or figurative names such as "The Red Lion" or the "Green Dragon," which were illustrated on their signs. This practice originated in a time when most men and women could not read and travelers needed pictorial identification to find their way. Some early American taverns continued this traditional practice, but in New England, where literacy was widespread from early settlement, it seems not to have been considered necessary. Taverns were instead usually identified by the innkeeper's name painted on his sign, sometimes along with decorative figures such as an eagle, a hunting dog, or a rising sun. By the late eighteenth century, named signs had become a legal requirement. State statutes generally required that a tavernkeeper who did not prominently display his name on his sign would be heavily fined. [8]

Foodways and Drinkways

At a well-run New England country tavern in the early nineteenth century, tired and hungry travelers would find a memorable welcome. "An hour before the stage coach was due," recounted Frederick Currier in his description of early tavern life in Fitchburg, Massachusetts, "the landlord was to be found in the tap room" preparing his bottles of liquor and "setting his glasses in single file." At the same time, he was urging the kitchen to "make haste with the dinner or the supper, of which there were already premonitory odors of the most appetizing kind." When the stage arrived, the tavernkeeper "hastened to the porch and stood there with a smiling face, the picture of welcome as the coach rounded up and the driver threw his reins to the waiting hostlers." [9]

In New England's cities, centrally located taverns by the 1820s had become true "hotels," which offered their traveling guests sizeable breakfasts and suppers and kept a lavish dinner

The tavernkeeper's wife was often the cook and almost always had the overall responsibility for food preparation. Wood engraving, frontispiece, in Esther Allen Howland, The New England Economical Housekeeper *(Worcester, Massachusetts, 1845).*

This tavern table scene shows some of the inexpensive English earthenwares that New England tavernkeepers used to set their tables in the early nineteenth century. Included are shell-edged plates, a painted jug, and a mug and bowl of mocha or "dipped" ware. The glass tumblers may have been imported from England or manufactured locally in one of New England's glasshouses. Drawing by Linda E. Peterson, Old Sturbridge Village, 1999.

table for the many merchants, lawyers, and clerks working in the city who could not travel back home to eat in the middle of the working day. In rural communities, this "walk-in" clientele was virtually nonexistent. Local men went to drink at taverns, but did not eat there unless they were in a dancing party or attending a ball — like the parents of Susan Blunt of Merrimack, New Hampshire, who, she recalled, would once or twice a year join other couples for a sleigh ride, a dance, and a tavern supper. For the most part, tavern food was travelers' fare, and much of what we know about it comes from travelers' accounts. [10]

Food and service at country taverns was a household affair. In architectural terms, all rural inns were just large

THE BALDWIN TAVERN.

Most New England taverns fronted directly upon a road. Occasionally, as in this example, a tavern in the countryside would be set back from the stream of traffic. Engraving in Elizabeth Ward, Old Times in Shrewsbury, Massachusetts: Gleanings from History and Tradition *(New York, 1892).*

dwelling houses. The tavernkeeper and his family lived in part of the building, and all household members who were able worked to keep the establishment running. The proprietor's wife was usually the indispensable woman in this situation. She was often the cook herself and had the overall responsibility for food preparation and housekeeping. If children were old enough, sons managed the stable and cared for the horses while daughters waited on table and made the beds. Otherwise, tavernkeepers had to find "help" and bring them to live in the household. [11]

William G. Buell's tavern sign prominently features a dog — in this case a retriever. Dogs were often found in taprooms and were part of the informal, sometimes rowdy all-male culture of tavern life. The game bird that the dog is fetching suggests the "bird suppers" that some taverns featured. Tavern sign, painted wood, c. 1820-1850, Old Sturbridge Village collections.

Travelers noted a number of peculiarities about eating in New England country taverns. For one thing, they did not serve meals at the convenience of the guests, as inns in England often did. Probably because kitchen help did double duty elsewhere in the establishment, they kept food service on a strict schedule. "At each house there are regular hours for breakfast, dinner and supper," the Englishman Isaac Weld observed, "and if a traveller arrives somewhat before the appointed time for any one of these, it is in vain to call for a separate meal for himself; he must wait patiently till the appointed hour, and then sit down with the other guests that may happen to be in the house." Another frequently marked feature of tavern meal times was the remarkable, sometimes almost incredible, speed with which tavern meals were consumed. Some observers attributed this haste to the stagecoach schedule; many passengers bolted their meals, they thought, because they feared that the driver would leave without them. [12]

Because country taverns were operated by households, tavern cooking was home cooking, spanning the entire range of rural New England foodways. Its quality varied greatly, just as it does in homes and restaurants today. Where the tavernkeeper was stingy, or the cook unskilled, the food could be awful. "The tavern at Shelburne Falls [Massachusetts]," Nathaniel Hawthorne noted in 1838, "was about the worst I ever saw — hardly anything being to be had to eat — at least not of the meat kind." In 1836, then sixteen-year-old Caroline Fitch found a "revolting" meal at Mr. Riddle's tavern near Manchester, New Hampshire. "The dishes," she wrote, were "placed at one corner of the table, on one of which were half a dozen pale potted pigeons with large white spots of flour on their breasts, on the other were a

few slices of meat in the form of steak which I cannot name. Miserable potatoes and a sorry apple pie were before us." By the time the entire company sat down at table she noticed that there were several more people than pigeons. This shortage did not concern Caroline, however, since she had lost her appetite completely. [13]

At some taverns, travelers noted that the fare was good of its kind, but amazingly simple. In smaller and more remote communities, breakfast and supper sometimes reverted to the most frugal and traditional patterns of the New England diet: fried corn meal or "rye and Indian" bread crumbled into milk. Writing his wife, Sally, from a tavern on the way to Portland, Maine, Salem Towne Jr. commented in 1827 that "my hominy [corn-meal mush] and milk supper will do now to sleep upon." In 1838 Hawthorne saw a group of young men, college

Factory-produced in England, mugs and bowls of mocha ware were inexpensive enough to be used in taverns — where breakage was common. Mocha mug, English, c. 1820, Old Sturbridge Village collections.

students on a geological tour, happily eating a customary children's breakfast of bread and milk — "with a huge washbowl of milk in the center, and a bowl and spoon set for each guest." [14]

Most tavern meals, however, were far more substantial — "generally plentifully served," said Isaac Weld. As Samuel Goodrich noted in 1832, the full-scale New England breakfast was "no evanescent thing," consisting of "ham, beef, sausages, pork, bread, butter, boiled potatoes, pies, coffee and cider." A modern nutritionist may blanch at

the calories and cholesterol such a meal represents (although it was being consumed by people who on the whole performed more hard physical work than we do today), but that it was abundant, even lavish, no one could deny. [15]

Some country taverns were renowned for their culinary specialties. The Tourtellote-White "Lower Tavern" in Millbury, Massachusetts, one local historian noted, was "famous for its bird-suppers." Landlord John White, "the most popular hotel keeper in town … was a crack shot, and always had a larder full of game birds." Others, taking advantage of New England's cold winters and the diffusion of knowledge about ice houses, provided their guests with iced drinks in the summer — "a luxury at table," the English traveler Edward Abdy said in 1834, that in Great Britain would not be found "at one of our best inns." William Strickland was delighted by a tavern repast "on a table cloth white as snow" that offered beefsteaks, lamb chops, freshly baked bread with butter, honey and

Made in the "pottery towns" of England, edged tablewares like this platter were the most affordable decorated wares available to Americans throughout most of the nineteenth century. Small shell-edged platter, marked "Stevenson, Cobridge, England," c. 1816-30, Old Sturbridge Village collections.

preserves, pickled relishes and pies; "such a scene gladdened our hearts," he wrote, "we praised American fare and enjoyed a meal so well suited to our stomachs." Strickland also noted, after staying at Frederick Bull's tavern in Hartford, that he "sat down to as good a dinner, and of as various dishes and as well dressed, as a principal Inn on a great road in England would have afforded, indeed, no man need wish for better entertainment." [16]

At smaller taverns, guests were often served together at a single long table — a practice that kept stagecoach passengers in continuing proximity and brought strangers into close contact. At other times, arrangements were made to seat parties or even single individuals separately. In his numerous tavern stops while traveling through Maine

and Massachusetts, Hawthorne frequently took the opportunity to eat alone — a practice that allowed the reserved young writer to observe his fellow guests for his journal without having to converse with them.

Travelers' accounts can tell us a good deal about tavern foodways, but for other questions we must turn to the relatively rare records kept by "landlords" themselves. Ezra Beaman of West Boylston in central Massachusetts was one tavernkeeper whose accounts have survived. From the mid-1820s to the early 1830s he kept a detailed record of his tavern's purchases for food and drink, and there is good reason to suppose that his operations were typical of those of many rural tavernkeepers in New England.

What do Beaman's records reveal? Accounts with local farmers and drovers indicate that he fed his guests

Tavern diners in New England ate in the traditional American fashion — conveying food to their mouths on the broad point of the knife, while using the fork, with its widely spaced tines, to hold meat while it was being cut. Bone-handled fork, probably English, c. 1830; horn-handled knife, probably English, c. 1830-40. Old Sturbridge Village collections.

American men of the early nineteenth century drank far more, on average, than their modern counterparts. Before the temperance movement became powerful, most New Englanders saw alcohol as giving men the fortification they needed to get through a hard day's work. Much of this daily "dramming" took place in taverns. Merchants, lawyers, and doctors, as well as blacksmiths, farmers, and laborers, took a friendly glass together while talking crops, livestock, and town politics. They would also drink together to celebrate such noteworthy occasions as George Washington's birthday.

large quantities of beef, veal, pork, sometimes turkey, and a good deal of chicken. (Beaman called the fowls "chickings," suggesting that this was the common rural pronunciation.) Mrs. Beaman and her kitchen staff then prepared and served this abundance of meat and poultry as steaks and chops, roasts, boiled dinners, and stews. West Boylston was well inland, but the tavern also offered seafood from time to time in the form of salt haddock, shad, and codfish brought from the Boston markets. [17]

Beaman bought fresh and dried apples in sizeable amounts, most likely for the pies that so frequently appear in travelers' descriptions of tavern breakfasts and dinners. Perhaps because his own tavern kitchen was busy with other kinds of cooking, by 1830 he was purchasing bread and occasionally gingerbread from nearby households that were functioning, at least part-time, as bakeries. Other eatables, such as potatoes, beans, root vegetables, and "salad" greens, all presumably came from the tavern's own farm. Entries for substantial bulk purchases of coffee and tea indicate that the tavern dispensed both beverages in large quantities; sugar, bought in even larger amounts, went for baking, and for sweetening drinks both "hard" and soft.

A look at foodways, of course, tells only part of the story of the fare New England taverns had to offer. We must also turn our attention to what we might call "drinkways," realizing that drinking in company — almost exclusively by men and for the most part in taverns — was a very important part of rural New England life. Everywhere in America, men's per capita consumption of alcoholic beverages was at an all-time high between 1780 and 1820 — far higher than it is today. Until the temperance movement began to gain headway, all New England taverns had "rows of decanters on the shelf behind the bar" where the innkeeper or his barman stood day and night, dispensing drinks to locals and travelers alike. In the wintertime, every taproom displayed long irons called "loggerheads" heating at the fireplace, "waiting to be plunged into sputtering and foaming mugs of flip," a potent, rum-based drink. [18]

In those more bibulous times, ministers, lawyers, and doctors, as well as blacksmiths, farmers, and laborers, took healthful "drams" every day and regarded alcohol as a fortifying bever-age that helped men get their work done. Although forbidden by law, it was not unknown for taverns to open even on the Sabbath, during the noon hour between church services; "while women replenished the coals in the footstoves," it was remembered of Sutton, Massachusetts, "men wore a path between the tavern and the meetinghouse to get their 'flip' or 'gin slings' and then return to the afternoon service." During the week, farmers regularly stopped at a tavern on their way to the store or the mill, "drank hot toddy by the bar-room fire," and spent an hour or two talking crops, livestock, and town politics. By the mid-1830s, Salem Towne Jr. of Charlton had become an ardent temperance advocate, but ten years earlier he was still following the traditional drinkways of New England men; while warming himself at a tavern in Bucksport, Maine, in 1824, he wrote his brother-in-law that "the tea kettle is on, the Gin is drank, and I hope soon to be more comfortable." [19]

Ezra Beaman's records provide a good look at a country tavernkeeper's provisions for drink as well as for food.

His accounts with Boston suppliers and local farmers show that he took pains to keep his bar well supplied. For "spirituous" or distilled liquor there was brandy (fortified wine) and Holland gin (distilled from rye and flavored with juniper berries) by the gallon and New England rum (distilled from molasses) by the barrel. He also offered a more expensive variety of rum distilled in the West Indies; in 1824 the Boston importers J. and W. M. Stedman wrote Beaman that "we have selected for you one hogshead of high sweet flavoured St. Croix Rum. We think the best you have ever had of us." For customers who wished milder alcoholic beverages there were quart bottles of "Lisbon wine" on the bar shelves, barrels of "strong beer," and a virtually unlimited supply of locally pressed hard cider. [20]

Beaman also ensured that he had a steady supply of lemons — used, we can safely assume, far less often for lemonade than for making "gin slings" and "rum toddies," two potent and highly flavored drinks much beloved by New England men. The tavern's sizeable purchases of nutmeg make sense when we realize that it was the final ingredient (when combined with the beer, sugar, and rum already on hand) of "flip," another widely popular drink. The barroom must also have been a smoky place. Over the course of 1831, Beaman ordered nearly a thousand "cegars" for his patrons at a half-cent each, along with a box of much more expensive Spanish ones.

Although Beaman's tavern, like many others, continued to operate in this way during the 1830s and 1840s, the increasing success of temperance reform began to change New England drinkways and tavern life. A majority of the churches came to oppose alcohol use in any form, and the Sunday parade of thirsty men across the common, once winked at in some communities, ceased for good. A substantial number of country innkeepers gave up the serving of liquor, either acting out of growing personal conviction or responding to community pressure. "Temperance" barrooms, without their long rows of rum, gin, and wine bottles, became much more sedate places, where smoking and tobacco chewing declined, men drank coffee or lemonade, and alcohol-fueled arguments

disappeared. Many of these reformed establishments were renamed "temperance hotels"; in quite a few New England towns a temperance hotel glared across the common at a traditional tavern where liquor was still served. This was evidence of a deepening division in the community. Many New Englanders applauded the changes and happily drank their coffee and lemonade, confident that a great social evil was being eradicated. Others felt that temperance threatened to take all the enjoyment out of life, and headed to the "real" tavern for a rum toddy and a hot debate about the next election. [21]

Upstairs, Downstairs:
A Look Inside Tavern Life

What were early New England taverns like inside? What would a traveler have seen and experienced when stopping for a meal or staying overnight? These simple questions are actually not easy to answer. Travelers recorded their experiences selectively, tavern workers left no diaries, and tavern proprietors were too busy to write anything longer than a bar bill or a receipt for meals and lodging. Digging hard through the range of now-familiar sources — travelers' descriptions, reminiscences, tavern financial records, and a few paintings and drawings of tavern interiors — we can find some answers. The most informative source, however, turns out to be a legal document — the inventory of a tavernkeeper's possessions, taken after his death.

Reuben Munroe kept a tavern in the town of Shrewsbury in central Massachusetts, beginning around 1835. He had previously been a tavernkeeper in Worcester. His establishment stood in the east part of town on the Great Road to Worcester, almost on the shores of Lake Quinsigamond. When he died in 1841, his tavern was thoroughly inventoried as part of the process of settling his estate, leaving a revealing portrait of its furnishings and many clues about what tavern life was like. [22]

We can follow the path of the inventory takers as they examined and

The world of the barroom or taproom indisputably belonged to New England men.

enumerated the goods that were in Reuben Munroe's tavern — an establishment full of furniture, beds, dishes, bottles, and cooking equipment. As most tavern visitors did, they began in the "bar-room," or taproom. Here they recorded ten plain, inexpensive "common" chairs, a couple of "common" tables, an "old stove", and a wooden-works clock that either sat on the mantelpiece or overlooked the patrons from a shelf behind the bar. For light-ing the room, the tavern had an oil "lamp and reflector" and an inexpensive looking glass; extra illumination was provided by six small portable tin lamps. Reuben Munroe's best gun hung on the wall, with its powder horn — just as depicted in some nineteenth-century images of tavern interiors. On the shelves behind the bar itself were a dozen jugs and demijohns and an abundance of glassware: nine decanters, twenty-four tumblers, six large square "case bottles" of spirits, and seventy ordinary bottles for wine and other beverages. Another 100 bottles were stored in the barroom's closet. There were boxes of cigars, kegs of gin, and, in the cellar, barrels of beer and cider. For preparing drinks there were graters, funnels, bottles of bitters and essences, and a sugar cutter — a bladed device for cutting pieces of virtually rock-hard loaf sugar. Near the door hung a warm buffalo robe for cold weather traveling and the landlord's whips for driving the tavern's horse-drawn vehicles: a relatively fast two-wheeled chaise, a heavier, four-wheeled wagon, and a sleigh.

As for the taproom's walls, reminiscences and travelers' accounts tell us that they also displayed a profusion of messages, advertisements, and legal notices — "placards of stage routes, woodcuts of enormous stallions in prancing attitudes, and notices of sheriff's sales," as Francis Underwood recalled of the tavern in Enfield, Massachusetts. In the barroom of a Shelburne Falls tavern in 1838, Nathaniel Hawthorne noticed numerous handwritten notes tacked up around the chimney piece, conveying such messages as "I have rye for sale" and "I have a fine mare colt," along with "a quaintly expressed advertisement of a horse that had strayed or been stolen from a pasture." Oliver Wendell Holmes Sr. described country taprooms as places "where there was a great smell of hay and boots and pipes," along with "drinking and story-telling" and, he added, "sometimes fighting." [23]

The world of barrooms and taprooms indisputably belonged to New England men. They were places where men kept their hats on, smoked pipes and "segars," chewed tobacco, and spat. In Munroe's inventory the receptacles for use by spitting and chewing men were innocuously listed as "boxes"; New Englanders called them "spitboxes" rather than "spitoons." Dogs were also a frequent sight in New England taprooms. Hawthorne noted while staying at a tavern in North Adams, Massachusetts, that there were "a great many dogs kept in the village, and many of the travelers also have dogs." They were "always playing about," he observed, and "their tricks

Tavern taprooms featured bars well stocked with liquors and walls covered with broadsides and notices. Men in taprooms leaned against walls in "awkward ... lounging postures," lifted their feet, tilted their chairs back, slouched, and otherwise brazenly violated the rules of good breeding. August Kollner, watercolor, 1840, Chicago Historical Society.

This sign for G.W. Mowry's Hotel, in gold, black, red, and slate blue, is a fine example of the sign painter's craft. The rising sun has a strong-featured amusing face, complete with aquiline nose and heavy eyebrows. Strong lettering, gold borders, and five-pointed stars make this a sign that would have compelled the traveler's eye. Tavern sign, painted wood, c. 1820-1850, Old Sturbridge Village collections.

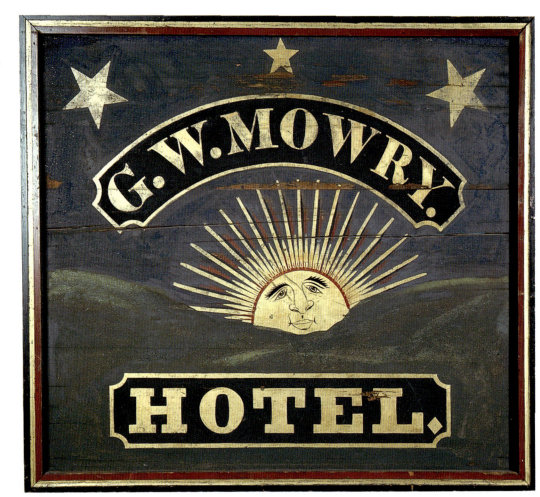

make much mirth in the bar-room." Such observations match with the spaniel depicted in David Claypool Johnston's view of a New England taproom in the 1840s, and the hounds, curled up on the floor or sleeping under a table, that we see in tavern interior scenes from New York and Pennsylvania. Animals appeared in places in the nineteenth century where it would be inconceivable to see them today; in New England dogs still often went to meeting with their families and sometimes accompanied them into the pew. [24]

Another feature of this male taproom world was the way men sat. Good breeding, as the advice books defined it, dictated an alert, erect posture, with feet planted firmly on the floor. Men in taprooms brazenly violated these rules. They leaned against walls and chimney pieces in "awkward … lounging postures of the body." As one offended observer noted, tavern-going men could not sit "ten minutes, without throwing [them]selves into … recumbent or semi-recumbent postures." They were "in the habit of lifting up one or both of their feet, and placing them on a neighboring chair. Others, if they can get a place on a sofa or settee, lay their bodies on it at full length, in a horizontal posture." And almost all of them, in one of the most "common peculiarities of

This 1824 sign for J. Kelsey's Inn features a punchbowl — an unmistakable symbol of drink and hospitality. Tavern sign, painted wood, Old Sturbridge Village collections.

Because country taverns were operated by households, tavern cooking was home cooking. However, innkeeper's wives and tavern help had to cook "for company" every day.

"common chairs" around the bar. A cushioned rocking chair, an expensive looking glass, two fine glass oil lamps, two fairly costly "card tables," and an upholstered sofa graced this space as well, along with "four window curtains with trimmings."

The third room, connected to the second by a pass-through that contained shelves and a closet, was similarly fine. It held a "dining table" and a more expensive "cherry table," and another eighteen "yellow chairs" only slightly less expensive than those in the previous room. Along with them were two cushioned rocking chairs, a valuable "brass clock," a summer carpet, two looking glasses, one with a "gilt frame," four glass lamps, and a parlor stove. Together, these two tavern rooms had an array of up-to-date and comfortable furnishings that would have satisfied the most demanding of travelers. They were also the primary rooms for eating, as was made clear by the dining plates, wine glasses, platters, fruit and gravy dishes, salt sets, vegetable dishes, custard cups, pitchers and bowls, knives, forks, teaspoons, and tablespoons that were stored in

American ill-breeding," constantly tilted their chairs back on their rear feet. Depictions of tavern interiors actually catch men in the act of tilting back in their chairs and slouching against the bar. No landlord's wife would have risked putting a sofa, or the best chairs, in the taproom. [25]

The next two rooms visited by the inventory takers represented the very different world of the tavern parlor. The second room boasted a set of eighteen elegant and expensive chairs, each of which was worth more than three times as much as one of the

the cupboards of both rooms and on the shelves of the pass-through.

Rooms such as these were sometimes called "waiting rooms," but more often parlors, or "ladies' parlors." They were designated for the use of genteel travelers, particularly women. As the Hungarian visitor Alexander Boloni Farkas wrote in 1831, they were often "tastefully furnished with different sofas, chairs and rocking chairs." He noted carpets on the floor, books and newspapers on the tables, "landscapes and portraits" on the walls, and "large maps of the best editions hung on roll frames." Here women could dine or wait comfortably for the stage, and men of business could write letters and plan their itineraries. The "waiting room" of an establishment in East Douglas, Massachusetts, was notable for a striking overmantel painting — "a view of the city of Boston in its infancy." Tavernkeepers often made efforts to adorn these rooms in other ways. In the late 1830s, Samuel Hayes Elliot noted of a well-kept tavern parlor in Connecticut that "in summer, fresh grown asparagus filled the fireplace; evergreens in beautiful festoons hung

from the ceilings and sweet-scented flowers stood within the windows, or upon the mantelpiece in pots of alabaster." Tobacco, spitboxes, and dogs were banned. [26]

Did one or both of these spaces also play the role of the "hall" or "ballroom" for dances and entertainments, so often mentioned in descriptions of New England taverns? Munroe's probate inventory does not give their dimensions, and the building itself has not survived, so that we can never be sure. We can note, however, that neither of these rooms contained any chests, cupboards, or other heavy pieces of case furniture. Their chairs and tables — and the sofa — could easily have been moved or re-arranged, and the carpet rolled up, for a dance, a meeting, or a performance.

Next, the inventory takers came to the Munroe tavern's kitchen. It was clearly a busy place, with two full-scale fireplaces (one may have been in an addition or ell that expanded the original kitchen) and work for two cooks. At one of the fireplaces was a cooking hearth with two cranes, abundant iron

One panel of the hallway wall paintings commissioned c. 1830 for the Howard and Saunders Hotel in Sturbridge, Massachusetts (now the Oliver Wight House at the Old Sturbridge Village Lodges). This panel depicts a lake scene with stylized trees, steamboat, sailing ship, and an island with small houses.

cookware, gridirons, a large copper boiler, teapot and stew pan, and a "tin roaster" and "tin baker," which cooked with reflected heat from the hearth. The other fireplace displayed the latest in c. 1840 cooking technology — a cast-iron "rotary" cookstove with its complete array of boilers, kettles, pots, and pans. Along with a worktable and a cupboard full of crockery and tinware, there was a lantern available to light the way outdoors, and six tin lamps on the mantelpiece to illuminate the room or to be taken wherever else light was needed. For the meals of the tavern household and staff there was an old dining table and six plain chairs; washtubs and half a dozen flatirons spoke to the endless chore of launder-

ing bed sheets and tablecloths, as well as the family's own clothes.

The census of 1840 for Shrewsbury tells us that Reuben Munroe and his wife, Esther, ran their establishment with the assistance of a woman in her twenties, a teenage boy, and a man in his twenties. (Their own children were already married and out of the house.) When the tavern was busy, with horses to be attended to, meals in progress, and rooms to be made ready, all five of them, and possibly others who came in by the day, must have worked hard indeed. At this point, the inventory permits one brief sidelight about recreation, noting that the establishment had four boats. It seems very likely that they were available for guests to take out onto the nearby lake. Weather and travel schedule permitting, guests who wished a little recreation could benefit from the tavern's lakeside location.

The Munroe inventory does not inform us how the entry hall was decorated, but we know that some taverns were remarkable in this respect. Innkeeper Ebenezer Howard of Sturbridge went to considerable expense to provide arriving customers with a striking visual experience. Beginning around 1830, visitors arriving at the "Howard and Saunders Hotel" (originally built as a residence by Oliver Wight and now part of the Old Sturbridge Village Lodges) were greeted by stunning (and still surviving) wall paintings in the front hallway. Painted in monochrome (black, gray, and white), a fanciful New England landscape covers the walls and winds up the stairway, with images of rivers and ponds, fields and trees, houses and farms, as well as a windmill, a steam-boat, and a sailing ship.

Heading upstairs, the inventory takers first saw a straw mat and lantern in the front entry hall and a "stair carpet" on the staircase. On the second floor they enumerated nine beds, each with a set of sheets and pillowcases (and one set to spare). The first bedchamber was that of the innkeeper and his wife; it was elegantly appointed with an excellent bed and bedstead, bureau, armchair, dressing table, washstand and bowl, looking glass, brass fire set for the fireplace, and the "sword, belt and brest plate" Reuben Munroe had been entitled to wear as an officer in the militia.

The inventory makes it clear that the other sleeping spaces, for guests and household members alike, were much more sparely furnished, and probably smaller. For all the remaining upstairs chambers, there was only a single small table and a looking glass; both were probably in the upstairs hall, along with the "night cabinet" — a piece of furniture that allowed guests to attend to necessary functions without going outdoors to find the privy in the dark. Five "tin reflectors" with candles were available for light. There were plenty of bedcoverings: six pairs of rose blankets made of white wool and decorated with a bright "compass rose" at the corner; two pairs of striped wool blankets; three com-forters, and five bed quilts. The decora-tive fabric "spread" for the beds included a "copper plate spread" whose fabric had an elegant printed design.

Virtually all sources agree that the frugally furnished sleeping accommo-dations of the Munroe Tavern were typical of those offered by country

taverns. However, the inventory does not make clear how the guests' bedchambers were arranged. Taverns seem to have varied considerably on this score. Susan Baker Blunt described a New Hampshire tavern that simply had "two large rooms upstairs; one was finished off nicely, where the lady travelers slept; and the other was unfinished, for the men when they put up there for the night." On the other hand, the Stratton Tavern of Northfield, Massachusetts, which was carefully studied by Old Sturbridge Village in the late 1970s, had its upstairs spaces divided into several small bedchambers for travelers. In none of these cham-

bers would there have been much besides beds and small tables. [27]

How many people would have slept upstairs at the tavern in its nine beds? That question too has its complexities. Before 1820 the answer would have been simpler. Tavern guests were universally expected to sleep at least two in a bed in same-sex bedchambers (except, of course, for married couples), usually with two or more beds to a room. Accounting for Reuben and Esther Munroe and the two young men and one young woman who lived and worked with them, we can calculate that twelve or thirteen guests could find overnight lodging. Thus the tavern could accommodate a full stage-coach load of nine passengers and the driver, with some room to spare for additional passengers traveling on their own. From the 1820s on, however, a few travelers were beginning to demand separate sleeping accommoda-tions — insisting on their own beds if not their own rooms. A coach-full of these fastidious individuals would have severely taxed the tavern's resources. More likely, the great majority of trav-elers who stopped at the Munroe Tavern were willing to accept "country ways" of hospitality.

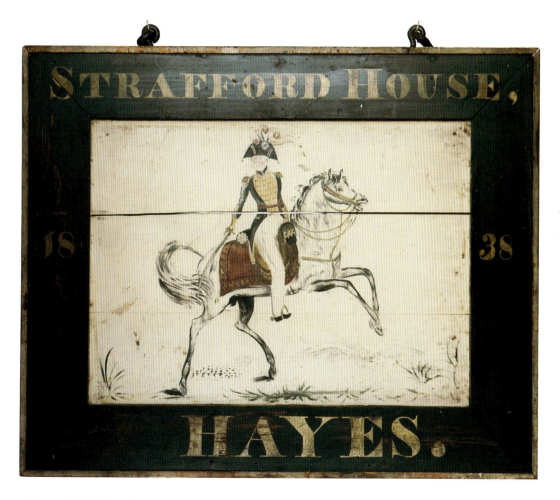

In 1838 Isaac Hayes, keeper of the Strafford House, had a two-sided sign with a different painting on each side. The soldier on horseback depicted on this side contrasts sharply with the bucolic image on the reverse. Tavern sign, probably Strafford, N.H., painted wood, Old Sturbridge Village collections.

'In all its crowd and tumult'
— New England tavern entertainments

" I … took care of the inn in all its crowd and tumult," noted twenty-year-old David Shepard of Chester, Massachusetts, in 1798. The son of a tavern-keeping family, he was living at home, trying to study medicine — and perhaps a little resentful of having to fill in for his parents when they were away. Sometimes the "crowd and tumult" were due to wholly respectable, workaday causes: selectmen often met in a tavern room, and it was not unknown for Justice of the Peace sessions to be held there — or even, as Hawthorne noted, a meeting of the County Commissioners. [28] Then there were the rare moments of sanctification. One of the most surprising sights New England taverngoers ever saw was described by Hiram Munger of Palmer, Massachusetts. Munger's friend, "Daniel," was a tavernkeeper in Tolland, Connecticut, who around 1840 was experiencing a long-delayed religious awakening and decided to turn his house to higher uses:

He had a meeting in the dining room at his tavern in the afternoon … before it closed, the bar keeper and others were on their knees for prayers. When their customers came in and inquired for the bar keeper, they found him in another room for prayers. … [29]

Given what tavern customers normally expected to see, this was indeed, as Munger wrote, "a strange and sudden overturn"!

However, most of the commotion in taverns was due to less weighty causes. The early American world was quieter than ours, without rapid transportation or instantaneous communications. By our frenetic standards, news traveled slowly and information about the outside world was comparatively scarce. Yet after spending most of their time doing hard and often monotonous physical work, New England's people were hungry for information and entertainment. In city,

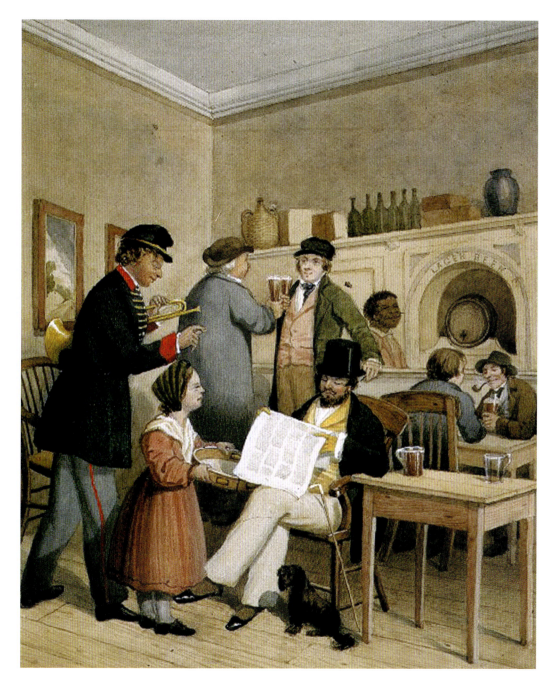

A taproom scene depicting men drinking, socializing, and reading. Two itinerant performers are also in the scene, asking for payment from a less-than-attentive audience. David Claypoole Johnston, watercolor on paper, c. 1850, American Antiquarian Society.

This 1836 view of Thompson, Connecticut, shows a family group in the center of the town common. The buildings facing the road at the right include two taverns whose tall signs can be seen at the common's edge. Wood engraving in John Warner Barber, Connecticut Historical Collections *(Hartford, 1838).*

village, and countryside alike, the tavern was one of the most important institutions through which they gained access to such things.

On the local level the tavern was the focus for talk, drinking, gaming, and sometimes dancing, but it was also a window to the outside world. In the years after 1790, Americans in the Northeast were busy creating a system of thousands of miles of improved roads, building tens of thousands of newly efficient horse-drawn vehicles,

and developing a far-flung network of stagecoach lines. Freight, mail, and passengers intent on business traveled along these roads, but so did a multitude of itinerant instructors, artists, and showmen. All roads met, and almost all travelers stopped, at the country tavern.

Entertainers

Traveling purveyors of popular entertainment were among the most interesting of tavern visitors. They also had the most marginal position in society. "Games, shows and entertainments" were widespread in early English popular culture and ranged from performances of Shakespeare and other dramatic presentations to puppet shows, sleight of hand, magic and ventriloquism, tight rope walking, juggling, trick riding, animal exhibitions, and acrobatics. New England's Puritan founders were deeply hostile to such popular entertainments and sought to eradicate them. The laws of seventeenth-century Massachusetts and Connecticut lumped traveling performers of all kinds with beggars, rogues, and wandering preachers, calling them all "vagabonds," and provided that they should be whipped, fined, and either removed to a place of settled residence or expelled from the colony. The official view of ministers and magistrates

The browsing deer portrayed on this side of the Isaac Hayes tavern sign of 1838 stand in striking contrast to the military figure on the other side. Tavern sign, probably Strafford, N.H., painted wood. Old Sturbridge Village collections.

This J. Brooks tavern sign prominently features the compass and square, a well-known Masonic symbol. Brooks was almost certainly a Mason himself and in 1824 was pleased to make his affiliation known. By the 1830s, with the growth of powerful anti-Masonic sentiment in New England and New York, such an image would have been very controversial, and few if any tavernkeepers would have dared to advertise their membership. Tavern sign, painted wood, Old Sturbridge Village collections.

was that such sportive, "wanton" entertainments took men, women, and children away from their work, worship, and community responsibilities and tempted them to even greater licentiousness. In the small and generally tightly controlled communities of the seventeenth century, traveling showmen and players seem to have indeed been rare. However, as New England's population increased and its links to the transatlantic world multiplied in the eighteenth century, entertainers began to appear in greater numbers, along with increasingly explicit legislation that signified their growing presence. [30]

In the matter of entertainment, New Englanders in the eighteenth and first half of the nineteenth centuries lived with a considerable gap between their actual behavior and what the law required. While in some jurisdictions the laws were becoming more permissive in the nineteenth century, the overall climate of regulation remained somewhat hostile, and in some states it was still flatly prohibitive. On the other hand, there is abundant evidence that many performers did manage to practice their trades and that many New Englanders paid to see them.

In Massachusetts, Maine, and Rhode Island, we can trace a change from prohibition to licensing in the first decades of the nineteenth century. The statutes passed by the first state legislatures after the Revolution kept all the old colonial prohibitions intact. But in 1805 in Massachusetts and Maine (which was then still part of the old commonwealth) and in 1813 in Rhode Island, local officials were given broad authority to license exhibitions and shows. In these relatively accommodating states, showmen could stay within the law if they could simply persuade the local authorities — although this was sometimes a difficult task. [31]

The other New England states were far more restrictive. In New Hampshire local licensing was possible, but the fee demanded by the law was $30 to $50 for each day of performance — large and seemingly prohibitive sums. Connecticut, the "Land of Steady Habits," and Vermont (parts of which were known as "New Connecticut") were even less welcoming. As late as

1839, Connecticut statutes still forbade "any company of players, or persons whatever," from exhibiting "tragedies, comedies, farces or other dramatic pieces or compositions, or any pantomimes, or other theatrical shows whatever." They also prohibited the public presentation of "any games, tricks, plays, shows, tumbling, rope dancing, puppet shows, or feats of uncommon agility or dexterity of body" and outlawed "any circus of any description" and "the exhibition of any extraordinary feats of any horse, pony … or any other animal." Vermont's prohibitions were slightly less detailed but identical in substance. [32]

These prohibitions, as well as the weight of official scrutiny in the licensing process, bore heavily on taverns, since they were almost invariably the places where entertainers stopped and sought to perform or to use as their headquarters. Tavernkeepers were sometimes singled out for special fines for harboring itinerant "rope dancers and vagabonds." Even in the relatively tolerant "local option" states, the authorities were usually suspicious of performers; the selectmen had the

power to license virtually any kind of show but often proved hard to convince.

Thus everywhere in New England, performers — and their tavernkeeper hosts — had to step carefully not to run afoul of the law. It is not surprising, then, that so many of the showmen traveling through the region sought to present themselves not as entertainers at all but as educators. Instead of Punch and Judy shows, performers offered painted scrolling dioramas that illustrated historic battles, Scripture stories, and the wonders of foreign lands; other entertainers exhibited menageries of exotic animals — not, of course, as vulgar spectacles but as instructive examples of natural history.

In Connecticut, it appears that for this reason menageries and dioramas were usually considered outside the scope of the statute prohibiting shows and were often allowed to perform. It seems likely, however, that less "respectable" activities such as trick riding and puppet shows at times took place surreptitiously alongside animal exhibitions. Vermont's legislators may

THE HAVEN TAVERN.

have been acting on this suspicion when they established a license provision for menageries as well; this allowed selectmen to license animal exhibitions at their option, provided that the proprietor paid a truly exorbitant daily fee ranging from $50 to $300! Officially at least, the Green Mountain State was that part of New England least hospitable to entertainers.

For a closer look at actual tavern shows and showmen, we can turn again to the observations of Nathaniel Hawthorne. Riding through the mountainous town of Lebrida (Charlemont), Massachusetts, in 1838, he reached a "small homely tavern." He stabled his horse "and entering the little unpainted bar-room, we heard a voice, in a strange outlandish accent, explaining a

Larger country taverns, like the Haven Tavern in Shrewsbury, Massachusetts, were usually long, rambling structures — the result of additions made over the decades as business expanded. Engraving in Elizabeth Ward, Old Times in Shrewsbury, Massachusetts: Gleanings from History and Tradition (New York, 1892).

diorama." Hawthorne investigated further and discovered that "he is a German, and travels the country with this diorama, in a wagon." Hawthorne joined the other men in the barroom to peer through the glass window of the diorama as the proprietor cranked a moving scroll to show them "views of cities and edifices in Europe and ruins; — and of Napoleon's battles and Nelson's sea-fights."[33]

On the same trip, Hawthorne met another showman, who was traveling from tavern to tavern on foot. The author had just finished supper in a North Adams, Massachusetts, tavern (larger and better appointed than the one in Charlemont) when "a man passed by the door with a hand-organ." Attached to the organ's mechanism were a number of wooden figures, "such as dancers pirouetting and turning, a lady playing on the piano, [and] soldiers" that moved in time with the music. Hawthorne noted that the showman "carried his whole establishment on his shoulder" and that "a little crowd gathered about him on the stoop, peeping over each others heads, with huge admiration …

all declaring that it was the masterpiece of sights."[34]

Susan Baker Blunt remembered a more impressive traveling diorama that came to the tavern her parents kept in Merrimack, New Hampshire:

One day a man came along with a show and stoped at the Tavern. He had a great Box looking waggon, with a door in the rear and steps to enter. I went in with Mother. On each side of the little room were little pieces of glass which we looked through and could see pictures. And on a shelf accrost the front end, little wooden Puppets would come out and dance. It was a very hot day, and the Man used the door for a Fan.[35]

Both of the tavern shows that Hawthorne described could have been officially licensed in Massachusetts, but it seems unlikely that they were. It also seems inconceivable that the modest show wagon proprietor recalled by Susan Baker Blunt would have paid a $30 New Hampshire licensing fee to stop at her father's tavern. Such small-scale individual performers may well have been below the level of official notice, or were judged harmless enough to be ignored by the local authorities.

Hawthorne also described a different sort of showman's visit — a time when the circus (that is, the menagerie) came to town and licensing became an issue. Staying at another western Massachusetts tavern,

Hawthorne watched the proprietor of a caravan of animals arriving "in a wagon with a handsome span of gray horses." The showman had left the rest of his troupe behind in Worcester while he looked for places to perform. In order to perform in town he needed a license, but the selectmen were at first unwilling to grant it, convinced that the show would only induce peo-

From time to time, magicians, ventrilo-quists, jugglers, and other entertainers stopped at country taverns. Richard Potter of Massachusetts was America's first native-born magician and a remarkable performer. He is portrayed here by Robert Olson at Old Sturbridge Village.

THE PEASE TAVERN.

ple to leave work early and waste their money. Both tavernkeepers in the village, Hawthorne noted, took the side of the entertainers — after all, they would likely "divide the custom of the caravan-people" for food and lodging, as well as gather customers from the audience. One of them rode off to persuade the selectmen to reconsider. [36]

From time to time, other entertainers who most often confined their performances to the cities — magicians, ventriloquists, jugglers, and "rope dancers" — stopped at country taverns as well. There were a few French, Italian, and British performers, as well as Richard Potter of Massachusetts, America's first native-born magician. These purveyors of acrobatics and legerdemain were often exceedingly skilled. Potter, in particular, was a remarkable performer. One New Englander noted that "Potter, the ventriloquist, visited the place to give his entertainments, which consisted of juggling, song-singing, legerdemain, and ventriloquism . … How I sought in vain to penetrate the secrets of the dancing egg, the ring in the pistol, and the pancakes that he fried in his hat without fat or fire." [37]

In the countryside such performers were often subject to great suspicion as "conjurors," because people did not always distinguish between wholly natural sleight of hand and the disreputable remnants of supernatural magic. Magicians were sometimes welcomed and sometimes ranked with vagabonds of the lowest type.

Traveling Artists and Instructors

Although taverns had never been renowned as temples of high culture, they did sometimes serve as artists' workshops. When an itinerant portrait painter arrived in an early nineteenth-century community, he stopped at the tavern, secured a room, posted his advertisements, and began seeking portrait commissions. Unless he paid in advance he might not always be favorably received, since artists were regarded with considerable suspicion. A painter who received fewer commissions than he had hoped might find himself in increasingly tense discussions with his "landlord" about the bill for his board and lodging. In July of 1824 the portraitist Nathan Negus faced such a situation and wrote his family that "not having a face to leave until I had paid my bill, my abode now became a voluntary prison … I shall not undertake to describe the wretchedness of my situation." On the other hand, if the tavernkeeper was willing to take his pay in pictures, tavern customers might have the opportunity to watch the painter in action. One memento of such an occasion is an 1839 portrait of then three-year-old Francis C. Babbitt, painted, as the subject later remembered, on boards from his parents' woodshed in order to satisfy the artist's unpaid tavern bill. [38]

Traveling lecturers and instructors shared the early nineteenth-century tavern scene with performers and painters. A few were teachers of fine handwriting, and there was a handful of learned speakers such as the redoubtable J. Evans, who traveled through Massachusetts in the 1830s (newspapers and broadside advertisements gave only his first initial, and they are so far all we know of him). Apparently aiming to satisfy New England's thirst for information all by himself, he offered modestly titled lectures on "The Earth, Its Productions, Inhabitants, Chronology and History, accompanied with numerous elegant drawings." A larger number were dancing and singing masters, men who sought to bring musical instruction and inspiration to the countryside. Like other itinerants, they made the tavern their starting point for becoming acquainted with the community. However, singing masters only used taverns as lodging places, because their primary concern was with the religious choral music of the meetinghouse. Singing schools never met in taverns; they were usually held in schoolhouses — because the desks and benches there provided the best accommodation for the singers — or occasionally in the meetinghouse itself. [39]

Dancing

Dancing was another matter. It was a widely loved and practiced recreation in New England, one that took place both in homes and taverns. Susan Baker Blunt recalled that her parents "would all go sleigh riding in a big double sleigh" with their neighbors and wind up at "some tavern for supper and in the evening have a dance." As she recollected, "every tavern had a hall where they could give dances." Rural New England's first and greatest social historian, Harriet Beecher Stowe, writes of couples riding off to where "a supper and a dance awaited them at a country tavern." In many taverns the hall or ballroom was a separate room, the largest in the building. It was often on the first floor but sometimes spanned the entire front of the structure on the second floor. In other establishments, a parlor room or two and even the barroom would be

As Susan Baker Blunt recalled, "every tavern had a hall where they could give dances." Tavernkeepers welcomed dancing instructors and were happy to host dances and balls. Renting tavern rooms to dancers and providing them with food and drink made for good business.

cleared of furniture to make room for twenty or thirty couples. For women who were not traveling, dances were the only occasions other than work in the household or official business on which they could legitimately come to a tavern. [40]

An abundance of evidence tells us that dancing was common, even customary, in New England taverns. But for Massachusetts, it also provides evidence of another gap between law and behavior. There, "dancing or revelling" in taverns was actually forbidden by statute from the time of the earliest colonial laws of 1646 until 1832. In other New England jurisdictions, only "revelling" — or disorderly conduct — was banned, not dancing itself. During the seventeenth century this prohibition appears to have been enforced, at least from time to time. Yet it is clear that by the early eighteenth century dancing was no less widespread in Massachusetts taverns than it was in Rhode Island, Connecticut, and New Hampshire. This prohibition had evidently become a "dead letter" not long after it was re-enacted in the colony's new code of laws in 1692 and

remained unenforced despite its continuation in the new state laws of 1786-88. Legal enactment did not match actual practice until 1832, when the section prohibiting dancing was quietly dropped from a revised statute regulating the licensing of taverns. Interestingly, tavern dancing was taken off the law books just when drinking and gambling in taverns were actually coming under tighter legal control. [41]

In Massachusetts, "dancing or revelling" in taverns was actually forbidden by statute from the time of the earliest colonial laws of 1646 until 1832. In other New England jurisdictions, only "revelling" — or disorderly conduct — was banned, not dancing itself.

Regardless of the technicalities, many young New Englanders welcomed the dancing master's arrival in their town. They were glad to have an opportunity to learn — for a modest weekly fee — the latest dances and proper deportment in the ballroom. Edward Jenner Carpenter, for example,

Fiddlers provided the music for most country tavern dances. In at least a few country taverns, a "fiddler's throne" built into one end of the ballroom gave the musician a comfortable perch from which to play. This handsomely carved example, from the Mack Tavern in Deerfield, New Hampshire, still survives. Currently in the collections of the Society for the Preservation of New England Antiquities.

was a nineteen-year-old cabinetmaker's apprentice in Greenfield, Massachusetts, and an eager "scholar" at a local tavern: "We had the first dancing school tonight," he wrote in his diary, "there was about eighteen couples there, it went off first rate, we had a livery team to go around & pick up the girls." [42]

Most tavernkeepers welcomed the arrival of a dancing master, not just for the money he himself would spend, but for the "multiplier effect." There was always a revived enthusiasm for dancing, and an upsurge in demand for tavern ballrooms, after a dancing school had been held. A look at Ezra Beaman's tavern accounts suggests that dances could be significant sources of income; the records contain numerous entries for "the rent of the hall and lights" and the payment of "admissions" for attendance at balls and cotillions. [43]

Yet not all New England taverns, and certainly not all New England families, welcomed dancing masters, or even approved of dancing. Because a high proportion of itinerant dancing masters were foreign born — often Italian or French — they became the subjects of ridicule by some members of the community, who thought them foreign, foppish, and frivolous. In 1821 the *New England Farmer* parodied the Italian "Signor Squeak" as a man whose "Dancing Advertisement" in the local newspaper claimed that he was:

> *A gentleman of vast agility*
> *Who teaches capers and civility …*
> *Professor of the violin*
> *And hopes to suit them to a pin*
> *In teaching arts, and fascinations,*
> *Dancing and other recreations* [44]

There were more serious grounds of disapproval as well. Just as those who continued to drink, even in moderation, became divided from the "temperance people," men and women who enjoyed dancing were increasingly set off from those who deeply disapproved. The lines of division were similar. Few if any of the new "temperance hotels" held balls or "cotillions," or provided supper and music for sleighriding couples. Clara Barton, who in later years would achieve fame in Civil War nursing and as founder of the

American Red Cross, recalled such a conflict within her own family when she was a young girl. Her uncle wanted her to attend a dancing school in an Oxford, Massachusetts, tavern, but her parents, much to her dismay, would not consent. The attitudes not only of families but of entire communities might differ greatly. Although the thoroughly respectable families of Merrimack, New Hampshire, loved parties and tavern dances during the 1830s, things were very different in Enfield, Massachusetts. "The country balls took place at the old-fashioned taverns," Francis Underwood remembered, and "were attended only by the worldly and irreligious," or at least so his parents thought, who forbade him to attend. [45]

In larger taverns in cities and county seats, a small "gallery orchestra" might provide the music for a ball, sometimes playing from a musicians' gallery or overhanging balcony in a two-story ballroom. But in country taverns a single fiddler most often sufficed. If there was a dancing school in progress the dancing master would play; otherwise a fiddler would be recruited from among the musically inclined men in the surrounding communities. There are also accounts of singers providing rhythmic "mouth music" of nonsense syllables for dancing if no fiddler could be found. The handful of known paintings and drawings of early American dance scenes show the fiddler standing near the wall or seated on a chair; but there

CHUCK KIDD PHOTO

fiddler's throne, a handsomely carved example from the Mack Tavern in Deerfield, New Hampshire, still survives. [46]

Songs and Games

Another cause of tumult in New England taverns came from customers singing to entertain each other. In the ladies' parlor, a convivial visitor might sing a sentimental "parlor ballad," such as a tune from Thomas Moore's best-selling *Irish Melodies*. But most tavern song was in the barroom, well on the vulgar side of the line of gentility. Local men might sing favorite old tunes, and passing travelers offered songs they had just heard in Boston. When the great Worcester printer Isaiah Thomas collected over 200 broadside ballads "in vogue with the Vulgar" in 1814 to preserve them for posterity, he was gathering up the texts of songs that were often sung in tavern taprooms. There were musical accounts of important battles and political events — "American Taxation," "Hull's Victory" — that to modern ears are long and tedious, and more sensational ones about recent

Card playing, along with other such technically illegal amusements as bagatelle and backgammon, could frequently be found in New England taverns. Gambling at these games was fairly common until around 1820; after that, men played them more quietly and "genteelly." In most taverns these entertainments were probably acceptable as long as no wagering was going on.

were better ways to keep tavern musicians visible, audible, and out of the tumult of the dance. In at least a few country taverns the solution was to build a "fiddler's throne" into the wall at one end of the ballroom. This elevated wooden platform gave the fiddler (and other performers as well, perhaps) a comfortable perch from which to play. One New England disasters, such as "The Dreadful Hurricane at New Orleans" and the "Shocking Earthquakes at Charleston." There were also ballads about floods, shipwrecks, piracy, murders, and executions, and a wide variety of humorous songs about domestic trickery and conflict, along with tales of outrageously good or bad luck: "The Lawyer Outwitted," "The Old Maid's Last Prayer," "The Deceitful Young Man," "Love in a Tub," and "Jonathan's Courtship." There were also many bawdy songs — songs never sung in the parlor — that men performed for their own entertainment. Some had innocent-sounding titles, such as "Corydon and Phyllis"; others had names hinting at their content, like "The Farmer's Daughter" or "A New Bundling Song." [47]

Amid the songs, some taverngoers were concentrating on games. As Charles A. Goodrich described them in *The Universal Traveller* of 1836, the games of New England were "billiards, cards, ninepins, shovelboard, domino, backgammon, bagatelle, checkers and drafts." Such recreations were a continuing preoccupation for many tavern-going men, but through much of the nineteenth century most of them occupied a shady border area between respectability and immorality. The legal authorities in New England sternly frowned on gambling or "gaming" in any form, and statutes on the books in all New England jurisdictions forbade taverns to keep "dice, cards bowls, billiards, quoits, or any other implements used in gaming." Yet these laws, like others we have noticed, seem to have been inconsistently enforced. "Gaming, especially the playing at cards," Sturbridge country lawyer George Davis recalled, was widespread in the New England countryside after the Revolution, and most rural taverns "had their recesses for gamblers." Davis thought that the rage for tavern card-playing "continued to prevail, more and more extensively" until about 1820. After that, "a blessed change had succeeded," almost certainly linked to the beginnings of temperance reform, leading to stricter enforcement of the laws and community pressure that banished dice and card games for money from the taverns, or at least drove such activities underground.

This did not mean that all games were forbidden to respectable men at country taverns after 1820. Dice and billiards, with their strong associations with gaming, were unlikely to be found in respectable establishments that wished to keep their licenses, but in many regular taverns it is likely that bagatelle, backgammon, and cards, although technically illegal, were acceptable as long as no wagering was going on. Backgammon, in fact, seems to have become quite popular with well-educated New England professional men in the 1830s; the young Worcester lawyer Christopher Columbus Baldwin several times recorded playing backgammon with friends, including a session that involved the Rev. Aaron Bancroft, Worcester's pre-eminent Unitarian clergyman. The main lines of division were those of temperance and gender. In temperance establishments, card playing and backgammon were unknown, but men could be found playing drafts, checkers, and dominoes — games that had never been banned. And at least in public, respectable women never engaged in any of these recreations; all of them, even the most harmless, were considered to be part of the male world of the barroom. [48]

Everyday Life in Transit

It is in the tavern, and not in the meetinghouse, that history catches New England's people in their most unguarded moments. Here we see them rushing for the stagecoach, standing up to the bar, watching a traveling entertainer, arriving for a dance, savoring a hearty meal, arguing about a town election, or trudging upstairs to a crowded lodging room with a single candle. The tavern was the focus for everyday life in transit. Landlords and locals, traveling merchants and itinerant painters, genteel ladies and the owners of taproom dogs — from the vantage point of the early New England tavern we can observe and appreciate them in all their complicated humanity.

Notes

1 *The General Laws and Liberties of … Massachusetts* …(Cambridge, Mass., 1660) ch "Innkeepers, Ordinaries .." [1647]. For recent overall accounts, see Kym S. Rice, *Early American Taverns: For the Entertainment of Friends and Strangers* (Chicago, 1983), and David M. Conroy, *In Public Houses: Drink and the Revolution of Authority in Colonial Massachusetts* (Chapel Hill, N.C., 1995).

2 *Badger and Porter's Stage Register* (Boston, 1825 and subsequent editions). For an overall account of changes in transportation and travel, see Jack Larkin, *The Reshaping of Everyday Life 1790-1840* (New York: HarperCollins, 1988), 204-231.

3 Diary of Caroline Fitch, 1836, Old Sturbridge Village Research Library.

4 Timothy Dwight, *Travels in New-England and New-York*; ed. Barbara Miller Solomon, 4 vols. (Cambridge, Mass., 1969) I: 309.

5 The regulation of taverns is documented in the published statute laws of the New England provinces and states. **Massachusetts**: *General Laws and Liberties … of Massachusetts …,* "Innkeepers and Ordinaries" [1647]; *Acts and Laws of the Province of Massachusetts Bay* (Boston, 1759) 10 William III, ch viii [1694]; *The General Laws of Massachusetts … 1822* 2 vols. (Boston, 1823) I: ch 65 [1787]; *Revised Statutes of Massachusetts* (Boston, 1836) ch 47. **Connecticut**: *Acts and Laws of the State of Connecticut in America* (Hartford, 1786), 240-244; *The Public Statute Laws of the State of Connecticut … 1838* (Hartford, 1839), 166-167, 507-509, 592-594. **New Hampshire:** *The Laws of the State of New Hampshire* (Exeter, N.H., 1815), 372-374; *The Revised Statutes of New Hampshire … 1842* (Concord, N.H., 1843) ch 116, 117, 118. **Maine**: *The Revised Statutes of the State of Maine … 1841* (Hallowell, Me., 1847) ch 36, 37, 160. **Vermont**: *The Revised Statutes of the State of Vermont … 1839* (Burlington, Vt., 1840) ch 82, 83; **Rhode Island**: *The Public Laws of the State of Rhode Island and Providence Plantations … 1822* (Providence, 1822), 295-297, 414-415.

6 Entries for "inn," "hotel," "tavern," and "public house," *Oxford English Dictionary*. Entry for "tavern," Noah Webster, *An American Dictionary of the English Language,* eighth ed. (New York, 1831); Jack Larkin, "Taverns in Worcester County, 1831," unpublished research paper, Old Sturbridge Village, 1977.

7 *General Laws and Liberties .. of Massachusetts …* "Innkeepers and Ordinaries" [1647]; *Acts and Laws of …Massachusetts Bay* 10 William III, ch viii [1694]; Edward Everett Hale, *A New England Boyhood* (New York, 1893), 187-188.

8 See citations in fn. 5, as well as Alice Morse Earle, *Stage-coach and Tavern Days* (Boston, 1912) ch 7.

9 Frederick A. Currier, *Tavern Days and the Old Taverns of Fitchburg* (Fitchburg, Massachusetts, 1897), 23-25.

10 *Childish Things: The Reminiscences of Susan Baker Blunt,* ed. Francis Mason for the Manchester Historic Association (Grantham, N.H., 1988), 24.

11 Currier, *Tavern Days*, 23; Thomas Fairfax, *Journey from Virginia to Salem, Massachusetts … in 1799* (London, 1936), 13.

12 Isaac Weld, *Travels through the States of North America 1795, 1796, and 1797* fourth ed. (London, 1807), 41-42.

13 Nathaniel Hawthorne, *The American Notebook*s, ed. Randall Stewart (New Haven, Conn., 1932), 61; Diary of Caroline Fitch, 1836.

14 Salem Towne Jr. to Sally Towne, November 17, 1827,

Towne Family Papers, Old Sturbridge Village Research Library; Hawthorne, *American Notebooks,* 61.

15 Samuel G. Goodrich, *A System of Universal Geography* (Boston, 1832), 100-101; Isaac Weld, *Travels,* 41-42.

16 *Centennial History of the Town of Millbury, Massachusetts* (Millbury, 1915), 372; Edward Abdy, *Journal of a Residence and Tour in the United States* (New York, 1834), 111; William Strickland, *Journal of a Tour in the United States of America, 1794-1795,* ed. J. E. Strickland (New York: New-York Historical Society, 1971), 93-94, 198-199.

17 Statements about Beaman Tavern foodways are based on Tavern Accounts, Beaman Family Papers, Worcester Historical Museum.

18 Ellen Larned, *Historic Gleanings in Windham County* (Providence, 1899), 162. For drinking in early America, see William J. Rorabaugh, *The Alcoholic Republic: An American Tradition* (New York, Oxford University Press, 1979); for the temperance movement, see Ian R. Tyrell, *Sobering Up: From Temperance to Prohibition in Antebellum America 1800-1860* (Westport, Conn.: Greenwood Press, 1979).

19 Salem Towne Jr. to William P. Rider, November 6, 1824, Towne Family Papers, Old Sturbridge Village Research Library; William A. Benedict and Hiram Tracy, *History of Sutton, Massachusetts, 1704 to 1876* (Worcester, 1878), 283.

20 Statements about Beaman Tavern drinkways are based on Tavern Accounts, Beaman Family Papers, Worcester Historical Museum.

21 See Larkin, *Reshaping of Everyday Life,* 281-286, 295-303.

22 Statements about the Munroe Tavern are based on the Inventory of the Estate of Reuben Munroe, November 2, 1841, Docket 42460A, Worcester County Probate Records.

23 Francis H. Underwood, *Quabbin: the Story of a Small Town with Outlooks on Puritan Life* (Boston, 1893), 15-17; Oliver Wendell Holmes Sr., *Elsie Venner* (Boston and New York, 1861), 65-66.

24 Hawthorne, *American Notebooks,* 40, 59.

25 Jack Larkin, "The Civilizing Process, the Conceptual Tyranny of Fashion, and Men Behaving Badly: Three Perspectives on Manners in Rural New England," unpublished paper, Old Sturbridge Village, 1997.

26 Alexander Boloni Farkas, *Journey in North America … in 1831* (Philadelphia, 1977), 85; Earle, *Stage-coach and Tavern Days,* 42; Samuel Hayes Elliott, *Rolling Ridge or the Book of Four and Twenty Chapters* (Boston, 1838), 98.

27 *Reminiscences of Susan Baker Blunt,* 23-24.

28 *The Chester and Westfield, Mass. Diaries (1795-1798) of David Shepard, Jr.,* ed. Alexander G. Rose III (Baltimore, 1975), entry for Tuesday, May 1, 1798; Hawthorne, *American Notebooks,* 55.

29 Hiram Munger, *The Life and Religious Experience of Hiram Munger* (Chicopee Fall, Mass., 1856), 77-78.

30 For several perspectives on itineracy in early New England, see Peter Benes, ed., *Itineracy in New England and New York* vol. IX [1984] of *Dublin Seminar for New England Folklife Annual Proceedings,* (Boston: Boston University, 1986). Also Larkin, *Reshaping of Everyday Life,* 204-231.

31 *The Perpetual Laws of the Commonwealth of Massachusetts … 1788* (Worcester, 1788), 347-349; *Revised Statutes of Massachusetts* (Boston, 1836), 400-401; *Public Laws of the State of Rhode Island and Providence Plantations* (Providence, 1822), 440-441; *The Revised Statutes of the State of Maine … 1841* (Hallowell, Me: 1847) ch 35, 39,160.

32 *Revised Statutes of Vermont* (Burlington, Vt.: Chauncy Goddard, 1840) 447-449; *Revised Statutes of New Hampshire* (Concord, N.H.: 1842), 239; *Acts and Laws of the State of Connecticut in America* (Hartford, 1786), 88-89,

161-162; *Acts and Laws of the State of Connecticut in America* (Hartford, 1805), 521-522; *The Public Statutes of the State of Connecticut* (Hartford, 1839), 166-169.

33 Hawthorne, *American Notebooks,* 58-59.

34 Hawthorne, *American Notebooks,* 55.

35 *Reminiscences of Susan Baker Blunt,* 21.

36 Hawthorne, *American Notebooks,* 51-52.

37 George Handel ("Yankee") Hill, *Scenes from the Life of an Actor* (Boston, 1853), 27.

38 Nathan Negus to his family, July, 1824, Fuller/Negus Papers, Archives of American Art, microfilm roll 611; reminiscence of Genevieve Babbitt Hardy. Both cited in Jessica Nicoll, catalogue entry, "Portrait of Francis Carlisle Babbitt," *Meet Your Neighbors: New England Portraits, Painters, and Society 1790-1850* ed. Caroline Sloat (Sturbridge, Mass.: Old Sturbridge Village, 1991), 69-70.

39 See Worcester *National Aegis,* February 10, 17, 1830. For singing schools, see Alan Buechner, "Introduction and Notes," *The New England Harmony: A Collection of Early American Choral Music,* Folkways Album FA 2377 (New York, 1964); Larkin, *Reshaping of Everyday Life,* 251-257.

40 *Reminiscences of Susan Baker Blunt,* 24; Harriet Beecher Stowe, *Poganuc People: Their Loves and Lives* (New York, 1878), 87; Stowe, *Oldtown Folks* (Boston, 1869), 349-351.

41 *Laws and Liberties of Massachusetts ... 1649,* "Gaming and Dauncing" [1647]; *Acts and Laws of the Province of Massachusetts Bay* (Boston, 1759) 11 Anne ch i [1711]; *Laws of the Commonwealth of Massachusetts ... 1807* (Boston, 1807), 374-382 [1787]; *Laws of the Commonwealth of Massachusetts 1831-1833* (Boston, 1833), 473-482; *Revised Statutes of Massachusetts* (Boston, 1836) ch 47.

42 Edward Jenner Carpenter Diary, Greenfield Massachusetts, 1844–1845, American Antiquarian Society.

43 *Diary of Christopher Columbus Baldwin, 1829-1835* (Worcester, Mass., 1901), 236-237; Tavern Accounts, Beaman Papers, Worcester Historical Museum.

44 *New England Farmer,* November, 1821.

45 Clara Barton, *The Story of My Childhood* (New York, 1907), 15-16; Underwood, *Quabbin,* 44.

46 Cynthia Adams Hoover, " Secular Music in Early Massachusetts," in Barbara Lambert, ed., *Music in Colonial Massachusetts II: Music in Homes and Churches* (Boston: Colonial Society of Massachusetts, 1984), 728-739 for dancing, 753-766 for music in taverns.

47 Isaiah Thomas, comp., "Songs, Ballads etc. In three volumes. Purchased from a Ballad Printer … to shew what articles of this kind are in vogue with the Vulgar at this time, 1814." American Antiquarian Society, Worcester, Massachusetts. These broadside ballads are discussed in Larkin, *Reshaping of Everyday Life,* 239-244.

48 Charles A. Goodrich, *The Universal Traveller* (Hartford, 1836), 38; George A. Davis, *A Historical Sketch of Sturbridge and Southbridge* (West Brookfield, 1856), 175-176. *Diary of Christopher Columbus Baldwin,* 254.